BODEGA

ICE CREAM AND
SODA →

CLOSED
DUE TO
POLIO
OUTBREAK

CLOSED

For Dana —D. R.

For Brian Forest —M. D.

Thank you to wonderful collaborators
Janine O'Malley and Marietta Zacker.

Farrar Straus Giroux Books for Young Readers
An imprint of Macmillan Publishing Group, LLC
120 Broadway, New York, NY 10271

Color separations by Bright Arts
Printed in China by Hung Hing Off-set Printing Co. Ltd., Heshan City, Guangdong Province
Designed by Aram Kim
First edition, 2021
1 3 5 7 9 10 8 6 4 2

mackids.com

Library of Congress Cataloging-in-Publication Data is available.
ISBN: 978-0-374-31391-3

Our books may be purchased in bulk for promotional, educational, or business use.
Please contact your local bookseller or the Macmillan Corporate and Premium Sales Department
at (800) 221-7945 ext. 5442 or by email at MacmillanSpecialMarkets@macmillan.com.

THANK YOU, DR. SALK!

THE SCIENTIST WHO BEAT POLIO and HEALED THE WORLD

Words by
DEAN ROBBINS

Pictures by
MIKE DUTTON

Farrar Straus Giroux
New York

Jonas Salk watched his neighbors pass by.

On canes.

On crutches.

In wheelchairs.

The polio virus had struck in his city.

Polio stiffened arms, legs, and necks.

Some victims even died.

No one knew what caused the disease or how it spread.

Everyone feared catching it from everyone else.

Adults kept away from bakeries and banks.
Children kept away from pools and parks.
People prayed for a cure, but who could
stop this terrible epidemic?

Jonas knew who.

He would stop it!

Few saw Jonas as a brave hero.

He kept quiet in class.

He could not run fast or leap high.

But Jonas knew a different way to be brave.

It came from his Jewish religion.
He dreamed of *tikkun olam*.
Healing the world!

Jonas vowed to stamp out polio.
He would do it by reading books.
Learning math.
And training to be a scientist.

He needed to think of something
no one had thought of before.
Something big.

Jonas studied science in elementary school.

High school.

College.

Medical school.

Dr. Salk buttoned his lab coat.
He was ready!
In 1947, he began searching for a vaccine
to guard against polio.

Scientists make vaccines to prevent disease
in the human body. Vaccines had beaten other
viruses, like influenza and smallpox.

But nobody could find one to beat polio, the sneakiest virus of all.

Jonas filled test tubes.

Peered through his microscope.

And grew samples of the virus to study.

He experimented with many vaccines but couldn't find the perfect mixture.

People heard about the kind young man trying
hard to stop polio.

Newspapers wrote about him.

TV cameras filmed him.

Children even sent him dimes for his research.

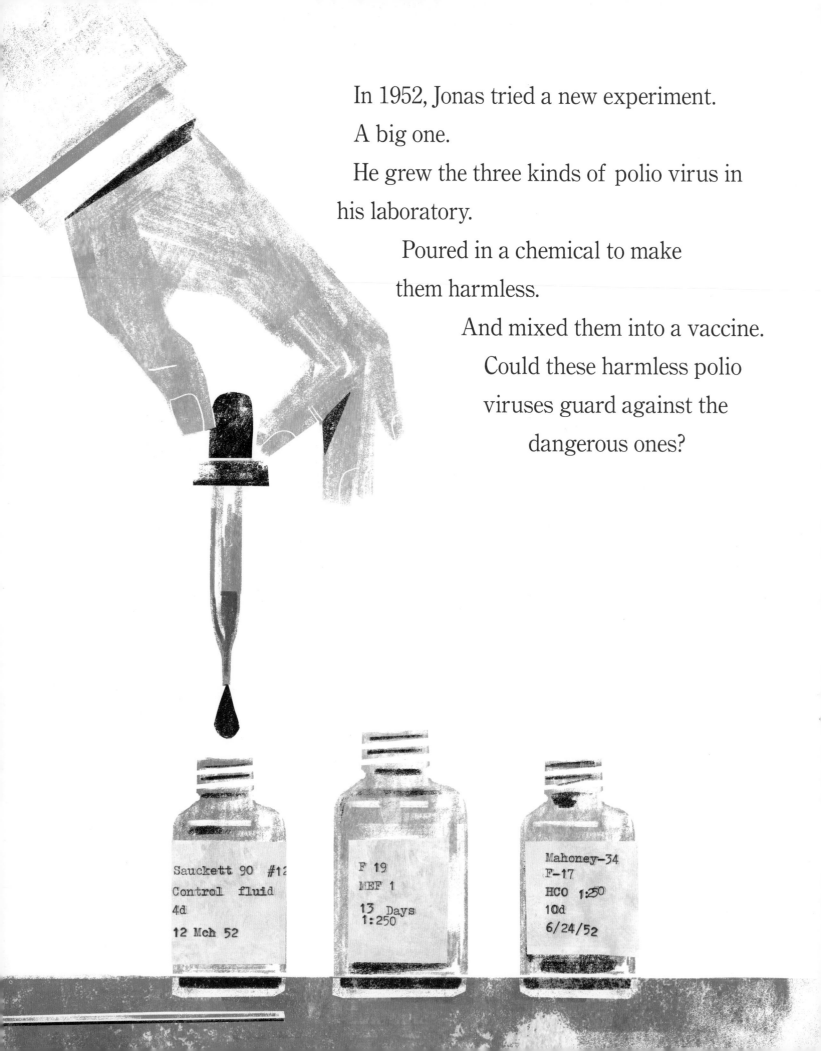

In 1952, Jonas tried a new experiment.
A big one.
He grew the three kinds of polio virus in
his laboratory.
Poured in a chemical to make
them harmless.
And mixed them into a vaccine.
Could these harmless polio
viruses guard against the
dangerous ones?

POLIO VACCINE
TRIAL

Please form
line and wait
to be called in.
Thank You!

Jonas tested the vaccine on a few brave volunteers, including his wife, his sons, and himself.

By 1954, he knew it was safe enough for a bigger test.

Two million first, second, and third graders lined up at their schools for an exciting adventure.

Doctors and nurses came in with trays of vaccines.
Parents, teachers, and principals served as volunteers.

The children rolled up their sleeves for a polio shot.

The volunteers gave them a lollipop, a pin, and a special card.

Everyone was proud to help Dr. Salk prevent the disease.

THE NATIONAL FOUNDATION FOR INFANTILE PARALYSIS

CERTIFIES THAT

HAS BEEN ENROLLED AS A

POLIO PIONEER

and this certificate of membership is

hereby presented for taking part in the first national tests

of a trial polio vaccine conducted during 1954.

Basil O'Connor PRESIDENT

Scientists spent the next year checking to see if the vaccine worked.

On April 12, 1955, they had an answer.

Jonas joined them to tell the whole planet.

The vaccine . . .
WORKED!
IT BEAT POLIO!

Cars honked!

Bells rang!

Adults danced!

Children jumped for joy!

Millions lined up for polio shots
at schools, libraries, and doctors' offices.

Thank-you letters piled up at Jonas's door.

One letter was two hundred feet long and
signed by an entire town!

Dear Dr. Sa[...]
Thank yo[...]
for helpin[...]
I did not like [...]
a shot, but it only hur[...]
a little and then
I got a lollipop. I hope
you get to eat one too.
Sincerely
Elijah [...]

Jonas did not sell his amazing vaccine.

He gave it away for free.

He said it belonged to all the people

who took part in the fight against polio.

Dr. Jonas Salk watched his neighbors pass by.

Adults headed to bakeries and banks.

Children headed to pools and parks.

They waved at him, and he waved back.

Jonas's dream had come true.
Tikkun olam.
Healing the world!

AUTHOR'S NOTE

As a child, Jonas Salk (1914–1995) saw many victims of terrible diseases on the streets of New York City. He felt for their suffering and wanted to cure them. He had learned the idea of *tikkun olam*—healing the world—in his Jewish religion, and he made it his life's goal.

Jonas studied medicine so he could prevent diseases through scientific research. He worked on a vaccine for influenza and, in 1947, turned to polio, a dreaded infectious disease that affects the central nervous system and spreads through food, water, and human contact. Polio paralyzed or killed millions of people during the early 1900s. It even struck the president of the United States, Franklin Delano Roosevelt, who lost the use of his legs. Because polio affected many people so quickly, the outbreaks were called "epidemics."

To protect others from the disease, President Roosevelt started the March of Dimes. The organization invited the public to join the fight against polio by sending dimes to find a cure. The money supported research by many dedicated scientists, including Dr. Salk.

Jonas acted more boldly than others, hoping for the quickest possible end to polio. After five years of experiments, he created a vaccine from an inactivated—or harmless—form of the polio virus. His research suggested that the vaccine would develop antibodies to protect people from polio without causing them harm.

Jonas's first tests were successful, marking a major breakthrough. That paved the way for a national test, focusing on the first, second, and third graders who were most at risk for polio.

In 1954, parents around the country allowed their children to get the polio shot, praying it would prevent the disease. The children were proud to take part, receiving cards and pins that dubbed them "Polio Pioneers." It was the biggest clinical trial in history.

On April 12, 1955, scientists announced that the vaccine had worked, and people celebrated around the world. Millions stood in line for shots, and polio infections dropped dramatically. By 1961, the disease had all but disappeared in the United States. Today,

80 percent of the world's population lives in areas that are polio-free.

I remember getting the vaccine at my St. Louis elementary school in the 1960s. I was proud that someone from my own Jewish faith had "healed the world."

Jonas had no interest in patenting the vaccine—that is, claiming ownership and earning money from it. He felt it belonged to all people who had worked together to prevent polio.

The polio vaccine brought worldwide fame to the modest, soft-spoken doctor. People named streets, hospitals, and even babies after him, and composers wrote songs about him. The United States government awarded him the Congressional Gold Medal and the Presidential Medal of Freedom. No matter how famous he became, Jonas still personally answered the many fan letters that read, "Thank you, Dr. Salk!"

Jonas Salk spent the rest of his life looking for other ways to heal the world through research, earning his place as one of the twentieth century's greatest scientists.

HOW A VACCINE FIGHTS A VIRUS

Viruses are tiny germs that can invade your body and make you sick. Scientists invent vaccines in their laboratories to help you fight off these germs, whether it's the polio virus or the coronavirus that swept through the world beginning in 2019.

Doctors and nurses give you vaccines through sprays, liquids, or shots. The shot might pinch for a second, but the vaccine protects you throughout your life. The protection is known as "immunity."

Vaccines contain the same germs that cause the disease. Not enough to make you sick, but just enough to help your body create a set of defenses called antibodies.

Once you have these wonderful antibodies in your system, they are ready to attack the real virus if it ever shows up. Antibodies are like guards that destroy the germs and keep you healthy.

Thank you, scientists! Thank you, vaccines!

VACCINE TIME LINE

AD 1000: Chinese experiment with preventing smallpox

1796: First vaccine for smallpox

1813: United States creates a National Vaccine Agency

1855: Massachusetts passes the first US law requiring vaccinations for schoolchildren, followed by New York (1862), Connecticut (1872), Indiana (1881), Arkansas (1882), Illinois (1882), Virginia (1882), Wisconsin (1882), California (1888), Iowa (1889), and Pennsylvania (1895)

1884: First vaccine for cholera

1885: Louis Pasteur develops the first vaccine for rabies

1896: First vaccine for typhoid fever

1914: First vaccine for diphtheria

1921: First vaccine for tuberculosis

1924: First vaccine for tetanus

1924: First vaccine for scarlet fever

1926: First vaccine for whooping cough

1932: First vaccine for yellow fever

1937: First vaccine for typhus

1938: The March of Dimes begins raising money to fight polio, and more than two million people send dimes

1945: First influenza vaccine approved in the United States, following research by Jonas Salk and others

1954: Schoolchildren receive Salk's polio vaccine in a national trial

1955: Scientists announce success of Salk's polio vaccine

1963: First vaccine for measles

1967: First vaccine for mumps

1969: First vaccine for rubella

1974: First vaccine for chicken pox

1977: First vaccine for pneumonia

1978: First vaccine for meningitis

1980: Smallpox declared eliminated throughout the world

1981: First vaccine for hepatitis B

1991: First vaccine for hepatitis A

1994: Polio declared eliminated in the Americas

2002: Polio declared eliminated in Europe

2014: Polio declared eliminated in Southeast Asia Region

2015: First vaccine for malaria

2015: Rubella declared eliminated in the Americas

2016: Measles declared eliminated in the Americas

2020: In the midst of a worldwide pandemic, scientists race to find a coronavirus vaccine

RESOURCES

Beckham, Michael, Richard Dale, Sarah Holt, Tabitha Jackson, and Gail Willumsen, dir.

    "Rx for Survival: A Global Health Challenge." WGBH Boston Video, 2006. DVD.

Colt, Sarah, dir. "The Polio Crusade." *American Experience*. PBS Home Video, 2009. DVD.

DeCroes Jacobs, Charlotte. *Jonas Salk: A Life*. Oxford, England: Oxford University Press, 2017.

Kinch, Michael. *Between Hope and Fear: A History of Vaccines and Human Immunity*.

    New York: Pegasus Books, 2018.

Kluger, Jeffrey. *Splendid Solution: Jonas Salk and the Conquest of Polio*. New York:

    Berkley Books, 2006.

Oshinsky, David. *Polio: An American Story*. Oxford, England: Oxford University Press, 2006.

Pemberton, Sonya, dir. "Vaccines—Calling the Shots." *Nova*. PBS Home Video, 2014. DVD.

Rosen, George. *A History of Public Health*. Baltimore: Johns Hopkins University Press,

    revised expanded edition, 2015.